Well On The Way
— A VIEW FROM 91 —
by Patricia Bradshaw

Patricia Bradshaw

ILLUSTRATIONS BY MARTY EVERDS

Illustrations by Marty Everds
Cover Design and book layout by Christine Delano

Printed in the United States of America

First Printing, 2011

ISBN 978-0-615-44177-1

To JANE

contents

| Forward

To write a memoir about old age occurred to me at age 86. This memoir would have featured episodes of "86-ing" (or dissing) us old folks, which was depressing and of questionable value. But, looking around at my old-ish friends, I was caught up short. One of them was 92, and she didn't make a point of it or fuss, as I was about to do-and am. I realized that I just wasn't old enough for an old-age memoir.

At 88 the thought reemerged, brought on by "*The Magnificent old 88's*" (an article about pianos, of course.) I was too young to be magnificent.

I lay fallow for a year or so, during which there emerged hundreds of Centurions. But also, suddenly, I became 90, to be 91 when the memoir is published. I looked at my glass and found it half full, and for the first time it felt I was at a legitimate launching pad, well on the way to that living Heaven of Willard Scott's jelly jars, 100 years old. I will be on TV for sure.

Join me on the way, with a version of Robert Browning's poem *Rabi Ben Ezra*, beginning:

Grow old along with me

The best is yet to be

The last of life for which the first was made.

Don't say "you Pollyanna, you". You will see my "bads" as well as my "goods". I don't claim more "goods" than "bads." Some days after a full glass of fresh, squeezed orange juice, I feel that claim to be so.

"Bads": I do belong to the cane brigade, and face up to arthritis every day. "Goods": A lot of the ugly events of my trip to 91 are in the past. My gynecologist has retired me, or fired me, and so has the colonoscopyist. "Bads": I have had two bone replacements, a hip and a knee, a lot of Mohs surgery, and, after another hair-line crack of my second hip, I spent a summer on a walker (the thing not the person) and ended up detaching my hip from my brain, which lends to Trendelenberg gait. Also called limping.

"Very Goods": I am regarding this phase of my life as travel into another dimension, not, I hope, just a small window in time, a calm between storms. I see no serious signs of Dr. Nuland's "*Ways We Die.*" I just feel lucky, with the "*Time, Strength, Cash, and Patience*" which were needed also by Herman Melville. I have plenty of time to read, time to actually think, very little pain, no insomnia, and a long list of things I don't have to do anymore. Think: throwing myself down a mountain standing on slippery boards. Although I have heard that some people are skiing at close to ninety, they don't have to anymore, to give the children the "advantage" of this experience, as we and their friends' parents did.

To me, skiing past the eighties is a weird form of Stockholm Syndrome.

So go on, Lucky, tell others what they should do to land here at 91 holding the glass half-full. Give advice; tell how you made salutary choices, and what you would have done differently if you had it to do all over again. I think that, as a Wise Old Owl, I should be able to do these things. But, strangely, I am not aware of actually making many choices. It all just happened to me.

Perhaps that is a customary feeling for every old person. Perhaps we make unconscious transformational decisions and attribute them to other people. Or to fate, or to chance.

But still, you will see what I am glad about and what I regret. And I will try to warn you of the "bads", those trolls under the bridge you are crossing at crucial or unexpected points on your journey. Since, remember, I have been there.

1 | Moving

We all diet; I because starving mice live longer. Every diet says, in one way or another, "plus exercise". Every dosage, every discussion of health, well being, geriatrics, happiness, being at all, says "exercise." If you stop moving, as fast as possible, or even slowly, if all else fails, you will get old faster. You will die sooner.

I did not exercise until I was 40 years old. Regrets, I've had a few, and this was a prime regret. All the health I have today I attribute to exercise. Why, when I had my knee replacement and rehab I discovered I was almost a different species from the others in my "class." The surgery is famous for pain, that rehab is the worst. I took a lot of Percocets, but comparatively few. I could do the rehab exercises—jam my heel against its leg to bend the new knee—much more easily and quickly than the others. I felt like a star, which is rare for an old lady, but very welcome.

If I had begun exercising as a girl I would have been a nova, I believe it. But I did get "C"s even in high school gym: when I brought my grade up to a "B" as a senior, the poor teacher sent flowers. (True)

My widowed, hard-working Mother discouraged all sports except tennis in which I got a "C", too. But, ice skating, skiing, no. Believing in what the then President of The University of Chicago said, my mother would quote him by saying, "if you get an urge to exercise, lie down and it will pass", or "walk to the library", depending on her mood.

At 40 it happened to me. I had been urged, teased, to join the so-called Women's Club in my suburb. (There was a Men's Club too, and a Chauffeur's Club in a clubhouse!) During the last adjuring phone call, I was watching a show on television with women in leotards and a trainer, and I said, "Does the club have gym classes?" laughing to myself. It was stuffy. Hats were worn before my hat time. There was a pause. "Why yes", the member said, "there will be. I'll sign you up." Thank my lucky stars, I began to exercise. Later on, yoga, with Clara Spring. During my 50's, I stood on my head, due to Clara!

"Yesterday."

I exercise, with more or less comfort and good sportsmanship. Face it; you have to. There is no choice. Kitty Hart, who died at ninety-six, put her legs up and over her head while sitting on the floor, most days of her adult life when she was not bed-ridden. She knew she just had to. She was trapped.

All this is fine; you feel better when you are finished, you feel safer, but when I stop to think about it now, at 91, there is something I don't like about it. It has become a life-and-death matter. I think of something which has bothered me most of my life, the oubliette in Chillon Castle. Remember Lord Byron's Prisoner. He was chained to a post in the dungeon of Chillon. Less fortunate prisoners were introduced to the oubliette. Beyond a door in the dungeon was a short, moving stairway, which led, if you didn't keep it moving by intense stair descending, to Lake Geneva.

I can't forget the sight and thought, and, for a moment now and then, I feel like we are on that small stairway, moving or else. Life as an oubliette.

I move. Housework is the "natural" exercise for women, but it requires too much bending and lifting, too much back. The second most "natural" exercise is walking, though "natural" is not my favorite mode. I walk with a cane, so walking for fun or self-improvement is not for me, but even before the cane I would tend to trip and fall. As a result I have the greatest collection of pennies I know of, due to walking while scanning the street looking for something to trip over.

Also, I have been through some grim foot pain, due to arthritis, and, of course, knee pain. Both of these have left me, somewhat disfigured, but with minimal pain, one due to surgery and the other due to the fickleness of arthritis. In my case, after disfiguring part of the body, my arthritis apparently tends to rise to another part, like rising damp.

I do cardio, by unnatural heart pumping via the stationary bicycle, the treadmill and the elliptical machine. For the muscles

I do weights, crunches, and that awful thing called tricep dips, or damned-dips, involving putting your hands on a bench behind you and dropping yourself forward near the floor and back up again. Often. Three times a week, I can do three reps of 10. I should do more.

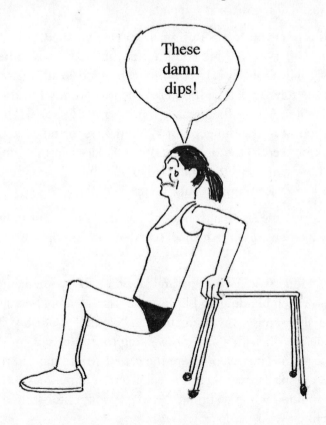

The more I do the better are my blood pressure, arthritis and stress tests. I am thinking of giving this last one up; what would they do to a 91 year old if she failed the test? It hurts to imagine, so I just won't.

Twister

Moving gets hard; arthritis doesn't go away. There are many ways I can't move now. A common complaint is the back zipper. I can't push my arms in place to lower or raise the back zipper. Call the doorman? Sleep in the dress? Wait until some woman enters your life? Play Twister.

Shoes. I can put on sneakers or their ilk on days when I have been eating very lightly or ignoring the universal adjuration to drink more water. You have to sit, bend over to the floor to deal with your shoes. It is better to do it before breakfast.

But, a lot of my shoe collection----my shoes are "collect-ibles"---- consists of middle-strapped shoes, with the major strap fastening on the outsides of the feet. Looking handsome and safe, since all those straps prevent your slipping out of your shoes. But, how can you reach down and twist across the body, breathless, long enough to push a tiny strap through a tiny opening? It is impossible.

Ask a friend to buckle your shoes? What friend would last? Ask a doorman to kneel at your feet? Never. Not P.C. Play Twister.

Pantyhose, the world's worst invention for people who can't easily bend knees to chest while sitting. One leg maybe, but my operated leg doesn't bend as well. To get hose on that leg, I have to fall over onto my back and find the leg over the body bending more easily. Twister. Can you picture it? Give up pantyhose and exhume garter belts? Double never.

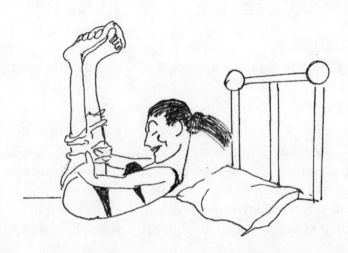

2 | Forgetting

Talk about regrets! But, it just happened to me.

Have you ever heard a conversation with no proper nouns? Like this: "Do you happen to know---oops, it's happening again, I forgot his name. It's that man from---oh, shoot---from where? I've forgotten but I'll think of it. Well, he's a lawyer, of course every-body's a lawyer, not a criminal lawyer, oh damn. Wait, wait, he was at that cocktail party where we both were. I think he has that disease where you shake. Maybe not. I'm sorry, forget it. When I think of it I'll get back to you. Or-ha-ha---do you want to wait until I receive a printout with the information-ha- ha? Or let me just go through the alphabet. Well, see you later." If they'd just wait, the alphabet sometimes works.

I do forget everything. It's that bad, worse when I get tired, pret-ty good in the early morning and after a nap. No naps, no nouns.

It ruins jokes and anecdotes. You just get the floor, everybody is looking at you, and you begin: "A woman is lying on her rooftop in the nude, sunbathing. On the other side of the park was the... well-known, uh, well, well-known to everybody but me, I guess. You know, blue and red tights, flies, you know. He's talking to his friend, well another with super powers-okay, it's of course, the first man is of course Superman. The other guy is, you know who it is, his pal, well, he doesn't feel like flying today. Superman takes off for a little trip around the city (also famous, but I can't think of its name). He wants to know how things are going, if the city is peaceful.

The friend waits and waits, a little concerned and mad, but finally Superman lands gracefully back upon the roof, and he's happy and laughing. The friend is really annoyed by now. It's been almost an hour. He says, "Who do you think you are, keeping me waiting all this time?" Superman lets this pass although he knows perfectly well who he is, and says, "Well, it was worth it, you'll forgive me when you hear. I was winging all over the town, and all of a sudden I saw a beautiful woman lying on her stomach on a rooftop, taking the sun in her altogether. Well, what do you think I did? I swooped down on her with the idea of great surprise. Superman, after all."

"Well," said the friend, "was she surprised? How did it work?" "Well, she wasn't as surprised as---oh lord, I can't think of his name. Oh you know, it's one of them. It has to be this man---oh damn, there goes my best joke."

A friend of mine in the audience leaned over to me and whispered: "Invisible Man" he said.

Nomenclatura

In ancient Rome there was a functionary who could be used by political hopefuls in their campaigns, know as a nomenclator. He was a collector and rememberer of peoples' names. An indispensable man, for politicians. I just hope poor housewives got to use him, too…

Forgetting for Good

Many studies are being done of the brain and memory. One idea is to eliminate some of our memories purposely, those that are painful---especially those laden with fear and trauma that occur in post-traumatic stress disorder. I am not a soldier, but I do relive some memories that make me miserable. Now, there seems to be help for both soldiers and me.

Dutch researchers have found that an old blood pressure drug called propranolol can rewire memory circuits to get rid of anxieties and bad memories. The drug is a beta-blocker, which not only suppresses strong physical response to stress, but also appears to retrain the brain not to react to a bad memory, and may actually weaken the memory itself.

Well, here come new meds, and here come the white rats, and it won't happen in time to control my dreams. It will certainly help soldiers of the future, and sad civies as well.

I saved this poem a few years ago, considered it for my Christ-
mas card. In the end I didn't want to seem so far "out of it", but it is
true. (Note the line, "his inner weather of pure meaning".)

Aphasia

His signs flick off.
His names of birds
and his beautiful words—
eleemosynary, fir, cinerarium, reckless—
skip like pearls from a snapped necklace
scattering over linoleum.

His thinking won't
venture out of his mouth.
His grammar heads south.
Pathetic his subjunctives; just as pathetic
his mangling the emphatic enclitic
he once was the master of.

Still, all in all, he has
his inner weather of pure meaning,
though the wind is keening
through his Alps and his clouds hang low
and the forecast is "Rain mixed with snow,
heavy at times."

----Vijay Seshadri

3 | Eating for Two

I have always been one who lives to eat, as opposed to eating to live. One of my few childhood memories I have is my mother saying to me: "Do you do that when you are out to dinner?" I said, "What am I doing?" "Kind of purring, but loud," she said. "Mmm-mmmmmmmmmm"

My mother made fried red tomatoes, chop suey, chocolate cakes on her days off from work. Oh yes, crackerjack on the Fourth of July. Otherwise my Grandma cooked. Mainly what we called beef-steak. Now, due to Liz Smith who says she makes it, it was chicken fried steak, with white gravy. Mmmmmmmmmmmm.

I have always eaten for two, not just when pregnant, but well before and after that. I ate to show my guests that it was okay to have seconds, there was plenty, and it was good. I ate to show my hosts that their food was good (mmmmmmmmmmm) and to teach my children mangia mangia.

I've been lucky. Oh, I have never achieved my perfect thinth, except in perfectly sad times such as losing mates, friends or relatives, when being thin doesn't do any good. But I have not been grossly fat. I have almost been on my second honeymoon, which lasted three months and did not count the calorie cost.

Even then, unless you looked at me in profile, I got away with it, and never bothered even to get weighed or to look at my profile. I only discovered my weight when we were about to take off for Bangladesh on a business trip. We were weighed in "stones." I asked what this amounted to in pounds and I found out. Horrors!

After our honeymoon I went on a diet, staying on one forever. Atkins, which works best, isn't good for you, and ten others were basically low-fat or low-carb, or all eggs, all fruit, or starvation.

At 91 I eat very little, more for breakfast and lunch minimally for dinner. That sounds good and healthy, but I don't manage to lose the last five to ten pounds, and I know why. Eating very little, I eat very well. Pounds of imported cherries at a sitting. Many cheese toasts with brie. Many BLT's with triple bacon, double mayo, and bread. Bread is the villain, delicious now with all kinds of grains and nuts in it. I always have extra toast. I eat pounds of "I Can't Believe It's Not Butter", which has no cholesterol, but also has a hook. I can't believe the calories!

I have usually excused excess spending by telling myself I don't smoke anymore. I excuse extra calories by telling myself I don't eat desserts anymore, which is almost true, which hurts, though not as much as no butter or sour cream, but it does not do the trick. Abstinence does, and I am slowly learning to use it. It has been said that if you don't drink, smoke or overeat you can live until one hundred. Or, it seems that long.

About Restaurants

I used to live to go out to restaurants. In New York or Los Angeles. I came to them straight from chicken fried steak. Straight to one called Lucca's and other Italians, affordable for students, where you got about five courses of what were to me exotica. To Ruby Foo's Den, whose food was better then I had years later in China, though it might be said that I didn't really know where to go in either NY or China or in Russia or in Germany, whose cuisines pleased me. Perhaps the Russian Bear? All of Yorkville?

I am glad that for a long stretch of my life, I did not know from chic. Without it I found the greatest French restaurant on Tenth Avenue in midtown called Café Brittany, and I have never seen its like again. I still miss it. Every person involved was French, all with accents better then my French. The food was simply delicious. I remember the cries throughout the restaurant "un vin blanc", or "un vin rouge." French sailors came off their ships directly to the Brittany, and we were all French for a day.

 These first places I discovered by myself provided genuine thrills, but after that I began to search out chic places, some of them wonderful.

Google won't give me the forgotten names, and I don't remember books of restaurants like Zagat in the 1950's and 1960's, though research might find them. I do remember the triumphant Le Pavil-

lon and La Caravelle, which were at the apex of self-indulgence, for
birthdays, anniversaries and other celebrations. I remember a book
called Blue Trout and Black Truffles, which uncovers the glamour of
those places.

Los Angeles

Google won't do California in the Seventies, when I was there,
but I remember two restaurants that were my clear favorites. One
was Perino's, a scene of drama like the movies. As I remembered the
waiters were liveried, and there were red banquettes. Formal posh
service.

Perino's status in LA society is attested by this anecdote. When
my husband and I arrived, for the first time, with our young people,
we passed by another table of a grandmother, her son and some
young people, rather like our assortment. My husband was obviously interested in the group and whispered to me "Do you know
who they are?" I was new in town; I didn't know.

As the dinner wore on, the other table began to collect itself to
leave, taking its time. My husband gestured to one of the liveried
staff to come to us, and he spoke very softly to him, saying, "Can
you tell me who those people are?" With surprise, but great dignity, he said, "That is Otis Chandler, and his mother, the *Los Angeles
Times.*"

The *Times* people gathered together and walked by our table to
leave. My husband said to them "Otis, I'm delighted to see you here,
And Mrs. Chandler." They smiled pleasantly, and amazingly they
knew our name, using it, when replying "Welcome to Los Angeles."

When they were gone my husband said "Whew, what a relief. I
met him at a Chamber of Commerce lunch last week." He gestured
to the waiter, and said "I do appreciate your helping me out there;

it was a great service." The waiter shrugged, and said with satisfaction, "Yes, well how do you think he remembered your name?" I had a feeling he was taking this story home to his wife and a wide acquaintance.

The other restaurant was where you went to see "everybody." After we began to know people, that is. On a Saturday night it was jammed, table-hopping was rife, and the chili was delicious. It was at that time presided over by the widow of the owner, Maude Chasen, and was, of course, Chasen's.

Now, at 91, the restaurant fever has abated. I like to stay in the neighborhood. I have a "local" I can walk to, and also a super almost-last-remaining grand French restaurant called Le Perigord. It has all of the things a GFR should have: waiters in black tie, properly dressed (no blue jeans) clients, cozy, well-spaced tables with gorgeous flower arrangements, brilliant table-side Dover sole de-boning and roast duck carving, knowledgeable wine stewards. Out-of-town guests who know I live near it, like to meet there, because I can cane there easily. I am no longer as hungry as I should be for Le Perigord, but should I have a depressed period, that French place alleviates it. Go ahead and indulge.

4 | Pets

I will tell you what you need.

Ninety-one needs pets for company. The children are all on
their own, and away, and friends are dropping dead all around one.
In addition, I can't explain why or be sure all 91 people feel this way
or this strongly, I feel the need to be connected to animals. I have a
lot of respect for Natalie Angier, a science writer for the *N.Y. Times*;
she calls it "reaching beyond the parochial barriers of the human
race to commune with other species."

I have a "relationship" with a small parrot in Florida. He is about
eight inches tall, colored gloriously in shades of red and yellow, with
a small parrot beak, which he uses for many problems other then
eating, like transportation. When he sees me he "acts out", hopping
from one foot to the other, ruffles his feathers, and squawks loudly
and continuously. He is a Conure, a breed very loud in general. His
behavior with me seems more extreme than his reaction to other
people I have seen him with, and his caretaker notes this fact every
year when I see him. This year he "danced" a lot. He is twenty-two
now, and will live to be 91 possibly.

I am embarrassed, because people can, and do, think of other
reasons why he acts out when I am around, but I just carry on
thinking he likes me. Across great time and space I think of him, as I
do other Florida friends.

Your eyes are rolling upward. You think I am deluded. I understand; I might be.

Birds would be an answer to our need; to me they do seem the smartest non-human species. But they can't be "trained." Wait a minute; there's a bulletin: I recently saw on TV a large parrot standing on the edge of a toilet "doing his business." An old philosophy quote is, "If it has happened it is possible."

I saw a trained turtle, too. Maybe, just maybe, lots more animals---all? ---are trainable, more than we've believed.

Anyway, now, before all the necessary studies are done, it just goes against the grain to keep a person in a cage. Dogs and cats are the answer. Dogs have faults, such as wet-nosing and licking people, and they are boisterous and careless. Outdoor cats bring in fleas and dead mice, and consort with other animals which cause them to catch ringworm which they can pass on to people. I have managed to live with outdoor cats with these faults.

I have had a dozen much-loved dogs in my life: a dachshund,

a poodle, a beagle, a boodle and a fox terrier. Each lived with me under perfect social conditions, which no longer exist. That is, there was a working family life, including for most of the years my four male children. These conditions provided a sine qua non for keeping dogs, namely a sure way to get them outside and back safely without my always going with them.

As time passes and 91 has loomed, it became obvious that indoor cats are my answer for the need to know other creatures and for the built-in loneliness of 91, so I have become a "cat person" by default. I don't like all cats, which a real cat person does, just as I don't like all humans. I don't like surly, standoffish, mean, dirty, cruel, and boring cats, or humans. In cats I abide unjustified pride and egotism so far, but as I get older I am less patient with both species' faults, including my own. The old don't suffer fools gladly, themselves included.

There is a (mostly male and odious) cat-hating for their supposed femininity, or perhaps effeminacy. Here is the real classic "dog person." These people are blind; do not see that cats are more male in personality than female. Independent, domineering, quite able to be alone. Very male, very cat.

I will tell you about the relationship of cats to 91, and not about the personalities of all my different cats. (If you like this kind of thing you should get a little book by the publisher Michael Korda and his wife called, "*Cat People*". I loved it.)

I am down to one small female cat, now. Ten years ago I acquired her and her brother as a gift. What a wonderful gift! I wish I could tell you all the clever things they did, and she does, but I promised you not to. Two years ago the male ran away while we were visiting a relative. His leaving had all the qualities of an escape, which nearly broke my heart and did break the heart of his sister. She still searches and calls for him, and frankly, she is bored without him. He kept things lively; he was a typical alpha male, who allowed her to eat only when he was finished, but he was good at games.

I have to fill in for my cat's brother. She likes to have me hide behind doors and jump out unexpectedly, to walk through the house trailing a long ribbon, and throw a ball for her to return. Sometimes. I thought this remarkable until I saw the Russian Cat Circus, in both New York and Los Angeles. The head of it travels with about fifty cats of all breeds and puts the lie to the idea that you can't "herd cats." Asked how he does it, he says, "I just tell every one she is the most beautiful cat in the whole world." I don't know for sure whether his cats are all females, but it sounds like it.

I wish I could tell you what his cats can do. Of course I can't. But, would you believe pushing dogs in baby carriages?

Standing in the flat of the owner's palm, up-ended in a handstand?

Walking a wire?

One thing I have observed about my cats: they all have a willing suspension of disbelief, which makes it easy to entertain them. For example, watching me put my hand and arm underneath the bed-cover, my cat sees it moving about under there and reacts as if there is something else under there to pounce upon. Maybe a mouse? I do hope not!

5 | All Those Kids

My mother, enamored of her first grandson, just didn't get it. "Why would you have all those children?" (She didn't say kids: children were not goats.) "You see how hard it is on Number One. He was so perfect alone." I thought he was still perfect, but maybe not.

"I did it for him" I would say, "to provide playmates."

"You didn't seem to miss them," she said.

"Well, I had you," I said.

The truth was that I was about 35, at the end of childbearing, when I finally realized what was supposed to be so difficult about being an only child. People said it was, over and over. That child, under at least semi-normal conditions, is an outsider to a marriage, one little helpless creature in the company of two all-knowing, all-loving-each-other-best big people. Wasn't this what they meant, not only, or not even the lack of in-house playmates?

My mother was, as far as I was concerned, always a widow, and, when you thought about it, she hadn't enjoyed having a baby enough to want to do it again.

She was all mine, at least when she was home from school. We lived with my grandparents so that she could go to college. And to get a Bachelor's and a Master's and a PhD, and eventually to become a revered professor. She was really in love with studying, or ambitious? I didn't know, or I didn't question it even to wish she would get me a father. She was perfect for me; we were all-sufficient, at first.

All Those Kids. We apparently didn't know what caused them, at first. It just happened. I couldn't believe it. I had made my plans for the future, following my mother's path. Graduate School, teaching, research, my first book, etc. Children, some time. I laughed, when I came across that schedule. I felt lucky that I hadn't actually been my wonderful mother, and I always felt guilty that I had not.

I had started bravely, working while pregnant, at Columbia University; first as an assistant study director at its Bureau of Applied Social Research, then as an assistant professor, with my PhD. When I taught, after my child was born, there were no women in the actual university, so I taught in the Adult Education School. I was followed around by an anthropologist at Barnard who was studying this rare breed---it was a long time ago!---women working away with children at home. Of course all fathers fell into the working-and-children category, but we didn't think of that very much at the time.

We had another baby, to play with Number One. Shortly I discovered a life-long belief in the importance of sibling position. I tried to convince people that all questionnaires, including the Census, should include Sibling Position. Just as often as Sex.

Number One was confused, then alternately jealous and overly protective. Once his little brother fell into a swimming pool—was quickly enough extracted—and Number One fell apart screaming and crying. Freud appeared: was the child identifying with his brother, or had there been unearthed a secret desire and fear of its consequences? Who knew? I felt it was important to find out.

There came a day, not long after, when our nanny stood at the door to say good-bye to the working mother, holding Number Two in her arms, with Number One pulling at her skirt, saying, "Come on, let's play!"

I shut up shop, and became a stay-at-home mother. I felt no choice, it just happened.

6 | Widowship

After losing two husbands, grieving forever, I sailed on unmarried. I always remembered my widow-mother saying "Ugh, those slack-thighed old men; I don't want them!" I never knew how she knew about the thighs, but my father was perfect, very much like my Number One Son, she thought.

But I had gotten the habit of men, and after a semi-recovery from grief, when my second husband died, I began to miss having dinner with a man. My first blind date was successful, friendly, we got to know each other quickly, and I said to him jokily, "Our marriage is impossible, you with your three living ex-wives and me with my two dead husbands. Neither of us could afford to take the chance." He agreed. He married again, but not to me.

Finally I spoke to a very popular friend, a widow, who was always out (or in) with a man or men, and asked how she did it. "Easy", she said, "you just get on to the walkers." I call it the Panel. It takes a while; you are new, of course, but just plunge in. Ask one of them to a benefit." "You're crazy," I said, "I was taught by my mother never to call a boy; it shows you are…a tart…or desperate for a date."

"Silly," she said. "These aren't boys; they're grown-up unmarried men (usually unmarried), and you're doing them a favor. Why, you know Pat Buckley used walkers because Bill didn't always want to go to parties. One of them came over to Bill's at the end of one season and dumped all the takeaway stuff they always give you at

benefits. The guy said, 'here, you deserve these.' Don't you see how
it works? They are happy to oblige. Usually they hire a car. I would
stick with those."

But, I failed. I chose an attractive man almost my age, literate,
funny, I knew him quite well, and asked him to go to a NYCity
Ballet gala, much discussed, touted to be glamorous. He was glad to
hear from me, coming from the depths of despair, and he said, with
no chagrin, no "sorry," "I am already taken." Taken! Ye Gods, this
was supposed to make me feel good? You have to ask months ahead,
and fight for them. My mother was right, and I wouldn't even be a
successful tart!

A man who lived in my building became a friend, just a movie-
going friend. He had known and loved my husband, so he was nice
to me. One day he asked me if he could come over and watch a
Knick's game on my TV, as his was broken. I didn't watch games, but
basketball was the least objectionable, as it had those huge amazing
leapers, so I said, "fine; I'll make supper."

That afternoon, an acquaintance called, a member of the Panel, and said, "Something has come up. There is a chance for a single woman to fill in at Mrs. Astor's dinner party tonight. I thought of you. It'll be great. There are a lot of theater people coming, you're lucky."

Wow, I thought. I could be launched, maybe into that fast set, maybe by-pass the Panel. "Sure", I said, "why not; what time will you pick me up?" "Well," he said, "that's the only problem."

I would have to get there quite unlike Cinderella, on my own. In a taxi.

I had forgotten the Knick's date. Never mind, my friend could use my TV anyway. I could fix him supper.

I called the Panel/walker back within fifteen minutes of his call, and refused the dinner. He was not amused, and hung up peremptorily. I wrote him a note, thanking him profusely for the honor he'd conferred on me (without a ride). I said "I could not love thee, dear, so much loved I not honor more," He never called again.

7 | Mom Knows

Remember the Jean Kerr novel and play called "*Please Don't Eat the Daisies?*" About her chaotic life with four sons growing up together. With daisies. It was hilarious. But, I noticed a small article on a journalist's encounter with one of the boys, who said "My mother's book was so exaggerated it was almost lies."

This impressed me, so I have not as yet written much about my chaotic life with my four sons. Or my husbands either. None of these males would have wanted to be "exaggerated" by me. Watch out for that, and don't get hurt feelings.

This said, the boys did dominate my life after their births. And do. I must at least suggest what it was like, so here is "Mom Knows," a dictionary game invented by my Number 3 son. He said that the cover of the "Mom Knows" Parker Brothers game box would say something like "Move over, Bill Saffire! Introducing Mom Knows, the rollicking game of high tension word play. Who thinks they know more than Mom? Could it be her two obstreperous, cunning, and highly educated older sons? Find out when you play Mom Knows."

The obstreperous ones, Numbers One and Two of our children, were to challenge Mom's knowledge of the English vocabulary. Our sons, Number Three (the game's inventor) and Number Four, were to select words to be defined, and Mom's four loving daughters-in-law were to judge and to oversee behavior. Mean teasing, insults and/or disrespect for the mother will result in negative points as determined by the judges, who will brook no argument.

If my referring to my sons by number reminds you of the older Mrs. Bush's referring to her relative Presidents as Number Forty-One and Number Forty-Three, I can't help it.

Rules: Words will be read out loud and spelled, if necessary, for the group by Three and Four. One and Two will predict whether Mom will know the answer. Additional points may be gained by actually providing the answer by One and Two. Voting "yes or no" correctly would be one point. Incorrect answers would be minus two points, with an additional penalty for voting "no" (implying disrespect).

This all came about because of a pamphlet assigned in a college class to Number Three, which he had left lying in his room on a weekend at home. I was "checking out" his room, and picked up the pamphlet and read some of it, looked up a couple of words in the dictionary, and failed to mention it to him for fear of being accused of snooping.

He then asked me about one of the words I had looked up, and then another and another. Millenarianism, then heuristic, then monitory. Of course I knew them, but recently. It could have gone on; the writer was, like Bill Buckley, a sesquipedalian!

"Wow, Mom, you just knew those words I have never seen before, I can't believe it!"

I began to feel pretty guilty, in addition to enjoying my status up-tick, so I had to level with him about the whole thing. There went the status up-tick, I assumed.

It didn't though. He was impressed that I knew those words even though I had to look them up. He shook his head, as if in disbelief. "You know a lot of words. We (the erstwhile "us kids") have always noticed that. Remember 'hyperphonating'?"

I said, "Well, with four boys in the family, we needed some protection from the F word, you know, the one that rhymes with heart." (Their father had perhaps invented this necessary word, as I haven't found it in the dictionary.)

"Well yeah, and ecdysiast and falderal and, and, oh adventitious. I used to get points with other kids from those words; not big points, of course, for just words. Of course I'll never forget when you told me I was rebarbative. Thanks, Mom, for the memory."

I had no idea that this conversation would result in such a big part of our family life. The actual play of the game did not begin smoothly. There was much discussion of who could be expected to know various words. (E.g. one of them wanted to be a geologist, so he would know "shale" and all its cousins.)

Three of the boys were in college or grad school, one still in high school, and that one was miffed that he was "out of it". Of course he got to choose words, along with Number Three, who said that that was no small thing, indeed. Four then would choose what seemed to be particularly esoteric and vicious words which did boggle everyone's minds. And, of course, the choice of "Mom Doesn't Know" might make her feel undervalued.

Here we saw the sub-plot of the game, or sub-plots designed to reveal the sib-stresses of the family. Would ex-game advantages or disadvantages figure in? For example, the sheer competitive fun of knocking Mom off her throne, not to mention the usual semi-serious competition between One and Two, which always existed. Also there was the "little one" status of Number Four, which we saw early on strongly affected him, and also the "big boys---little boys" dynamic. Unfortunately, this was based on the younger boys' being left behind on major trips, and on other experiences like earlier bedtimes, tastes of wine, excuses from Sunday School, which permanently tainted their adult relationships. Decreasingly, I found, as they grew up, and best friendships changed or moved around, usually happily.

Mom Knows became, I have to say, a drinking game, increasingly, and sometimes rowdy. It was a lot of fun, and we play it on the rarer and rarer occasions when we are altogether in one place and time.

Alas, Mom doesn't often know anymore. I forget my vocabulary, resort to synonyms, or "you know what I mean". It has been suggested that we promote Numbers One and Two to be Kings whom we strive to topple, but this plan never worked out.

On the whole, the game was a plus for the family, one reason being that there came a time when Number Four, the "little one" (now fifty-six) clearly triumphed. Number Three picked an odd, unusually short word, "arête", which left One and Two cold. All threw up their hands. It was the end of a game, and someone asked me if I knew what it meant. I said no, but Four stood up and pointed at me. "Yes you do too know, I told you, a long time ago when we were trying to name our new boat. I said it ought to be "arête", which means "virtue", but it is a word in Greek. It may be spelled "areti," too. Arête's in our dictionary in English; it means something like a ridge or a sharp mountain, but we had a Greek kid in a class where we were talking about ethics and he told us about arête, in Greek, virtue....see?"

Did Number Three see? Is that why he chose "arête"? I like to think so. There was a general, long-in-coming applause.

8 | Famous People I Have Been Close To

Would you believe the astronauts, all of them, including the Walkers on the Moon, John Glenn, Gus Grisom, Neil Armstrong, all of them? Some people know the senator; some know one or two others. But I...well I...must have The Right Stuff.

What happened was that I lived in the neighborhood of Cal Tech; I knew a few professors there and many of the Cal Tech wives. They got to know me, and my outstanding, huge kidney-shaped swimming pool. It had been built by a very happy and playful inventor and his pelf, and had varieties of splendid toys, which bespoke a family of children and child-like adults. For example, there was a long, curved slide, which began at the door of the master bedroom and (lavishly watered) ended in the pool below. There was an outsized trampoline on the side overlooking and very near a six-foot drop into a canyon, which was in the city of San Marino, while the rest of the property was in Pasadena. Nearby was a long scary diving board, and a lot of glamorous and unusual poolside lounging furniture. We had bought the outdoors furnished.

Because of this spectacular pool I was elected to entertain the astronauts, who were convening (all of them, many with wives) at Cal Tech. In the middle of the convention they were to have a day off, a splendid picnic organized by the Cal Tech wives. Kegs of beer, piped in music, hamburgers, hot dogs, sweet corn, salads, ice cream, watermelon. Well, the American barbeque "works."

Would I have them? I would. I was thrilled to. A person who

wouldn't bother to meet Aristotle, because I didn't speak ancient Greek, a person who lied about not wanting to meet Hollywood celebs, because that wasn't cool. I would want to meet men who made it to the moon. Could I ask a couple of my California sons?

The blow fell, too late to back out. I had already said "yes" And 'yes, yes' again, when I heard that they wanted my pool but not me. None of my family was to greet them; I wasn't to even see them, not to impose. To actually go away. They were to be free to enjoy a day with no obligations to answer to anyone.

Mi casa es su casa!

I disappeared that day when the beer and cokes came through my gate. But, I did have an ace in the hole. Picture the pool; picture the structure above the pool, running from the master bedroom door and around the pool. Three rooms: a ladies dressing room, with facilities, and then a long room covered with darkened glass, which the inventor had conceived for himself---he could see out but no one could see him and his work inside, a huge office/workroom, which now held my computer, my files, my sewing machine, my hair dryer. I had flipped a coin with my husband for this room and lost, but he really didn't think some of my machines fit into the house proper, so I won it in the end.

Attached to that room was a men's dressing room, with facilities.

My ace in the hole was that dark room, into which I had sidled when the drinks arrived.

It was a long, long day, but an exciting one. As I identified each astronaut walking by in front of me, I would telephone one of my sons to say, "guess who just went by." One of them came very close, to go down the slide, bursting out of the water below with a laughing "Hey, try this, it's a gas!" A man who had been on the moon!

They all walked by the dark room, peering in, not seeing, and I stayed there glad to be free of the obligation to…to talk to an astronaut. Oh sure, of course!

After about 4:30 they began to hit the dressing rooms and then to shuffle off, sunburned. I may have fallen asleep during the grand exit. It was pretty quiet. All in all I felt pretty lucky.

Now would you believe Diana? The Princess Diana. Move with me into the future, another pool. A beach. Martha's Vineyard. I had them, she needed them.

When Diana was separated from Charles, she needed a new life, new adventures. The Clintons had come to the Vineyard. Lady Bird was there. Actresses and politicians were there. So it became a "destination". A venue.

She had decided a bit late; all the beach houses were either occupied by their owners or borrowed. With the help of a highly-recommended realtor, Diana rented a beautiful house overlooking a picturesque horse farm, surrounded by 200-year old trees, a tennis court, and room for many guests, beautifully appointed, and belonging to the chairman of Sak's Fifth Ave. No pool, no beach. Everything else, but not really Island-y.

The realtor knew our house, with pool, with beach. He came to me. Could she have my place for just two days, poor lady? One pool day, one beach day. With her two friends, a couple traveling with her. Remembering my decision to skip meeting Aristotle because of no Greek, you would think I'd skip Diana, not speaking English Royalty. But no. There were special circumstances.

One of my beloved daughters-in-law was an avid Dianaphile. She looked like Diana, with her little head tip, her curly smile. How she loved Diana. Oh what I would do for this Diana-in-waiting. Downing a fleeting specter of an astronaut—it couldn't happen twice--I gushed. "I'd love to have her. Them. Give me a few days to royalize my place and –luckily my kids will be visiting, the one who is a deep Dianafile. Oh, that will make me happy!"

Sucker. You should have known. They wanted my places, not me. Not us. I began to back off. The realtor played his card. At the end

of Diana's stay on the Vineyard, everyone who has helped to make
her stay memorable--and I would be the most, of course--what a
good sport, he knew me to be. He knew I would understand the
poor little thing wanted freedom from obligation. On her vacation.
There was to be a boat trip. The realtor's company had access to a
huge yacht. I would be invited, along with others, to celebrate her
lovely stay on our island which we had made possible.

"No, no, no", I said. I wanted my daughter to meet her, not me.
"Fine", he said. "She can go instead of you. With you. It will even
be better."

I was able to promise this great gift, proudly, to my daughter.
What mother-in-law could produce a princess? I could.

She was suitably impressed. Joyful, actually. Of course, there was
a bit of a problem with the timing. My son's vacation would not
encompass the boat trip, so he wouldn't be here to keep their two
little girls, aged four and six. But my daughter would manage, make
it possible, everyone would. It was worth anything.

The day before the pool day, I had gone to the market. It was a
quiet day, the store almost empty. Except for Diana and her friends,
and me, in the cracker aisle.

My heart pounding, I approached them, tried to identify myself,
hated myself. Finally, the wife said "Oh yes, you must be Number 1
Oyster Watcha. The place we are going to tomorrow." Diana looked
bland. I went on, rudely of course, determined, embarrassed, a
mother through and through. "I am so glad you are coming, so glad.
My daughter just loves you, she even looks like you, and she sometimes thinks she is you."

Diana smiled, a regretful little smile, and she said, "I wish she
had been. I'm sure she would have done a better job." With further
hapless words unsaid, with a lump in my throat beyond which they
wouldn't emerge, I beat a retreat.

The Pool Day took place. My family and I went to Oak Bluffs, rode the Flying Horses merry-go-round, had lunch at Linda Jean's and went to a movie. With two tired and nap-less little girls in tow we went home, late enough. Diana had left.

I called the realtor to check on the promised yacht trip, supposed to be two days after the Beach Day. He was so sorry; Diana had decided to leave us early. Something had come up. No boat trip. No daughter--Diana meeting.

I seethed. My daughter-in-law was hideously disappointed. My son had left, leaving his wife and the children with me. I gritted my teeth and planned a long day at (then) Gay Head. We would have lunch at The Bite, a famous little shack serving delicious clams. Mussels, clam chowder. Then we would buy gifts to take back home, souvenirs for the girls, remembrances. The plan was unsuccessful in advance.

"Another day acting like tourists, what's the use of having a home here if you have to act like visitors; I hate mussels, I hate clams," said the six-year-old, "I am tired from yesterday."

So was I. "We'll go to see the llamas, you loved them last year. And, and," I began to see what would happen. "We will come back early and have a swim in the pool before supper."

"I bet Princess Diana peed in our pool," she said, crossly.

"Oh, I hope so," said her mother.

The Beach Day. The last day. I was mad. I was furious. I was frustrated. I had been had, once again. Astronauts whirled through my mind. We would come home early, all right.

We skipped Menemsha and the llamas, concentrated on the trinkets, came into our driveway at three o'clock. The Dianacar was awaiting her. She was at the beach.

"Come on everybody, we are going to meet Diana," I said.

We approached the beach in an unusual way, through our front hedge, where there was a small, almost impassable opening to the

shore. We would be on the wrong side of them, unexpected. Me
first, followed by the little girls clutching their mothers' hands. There
was Diana, on her stomach in the sand, gorgeous even from behind.
Sitting in beach chairs were the protectors. No one else was near.

In the tense silence, Diana rose to her feet. I introduced us; one
of us attempted a wobbly curtsy in the sand. Diana, a perfect lady,
held out her hand to my daughter, smiling, apparently remembering
the wannabe, and then bending to the little girls.

Truthfully, as it happened in the market, I do not know how we
got out of there, or what else happened, but as we retreated soon
into the bushes, I, leaving all Aristotles behind me forever, swearing
silently, "Never again".

Amazingly, my daughter-in-law was overjoyed. She gave me a
big hug and applauded me, saying "Oh, thank you, thank you. That
was wonderful. Girls, we'll never forget Granny gave us a real princess, will we?"

Well, this was almost what I wanted, wasn't it? I was, of course, hu-
miliated. But this is a special case, which also happens. Should I have
stuck by my Aristotle vow or given my child pleasure? There is a choice!
It can happen, and I wish I knew for sure my choice was justifiable.

9 | The New World

It is true that the new world belongs to the young. "They" live in a different world. As Coleman McCarthy said in The Road "I am an alien, a being from a planet that no longer exists." My children live in this planet and my grandchildren, everyone texting, taking phone pictures, reading E-mails far away from their mother computers.

Well, aha, I'm not quite out of it. It so happened that I had an IBM personal computer called the Displaywriter in the early 1980's. Because IBM "made it available" to Walter Cronkite, who was an old sailing buddy of ours, I made it available to me, too, and I was hooked. I had a few other friends who had them—writers, as I hoped to be—and it was a kind of club. We would discuss our babies' latest achievements, incessant demands, and peculiarities.

The Displaywriter was freestanding, so very tall and wide that

I have often thought of what happened after their retirement; was there a huge elephants' grave-yard somewhere with all those beasts rotting away alone?

One of the first things that happened was a flood of material, to which I had subscribed and which added to itself, piling up in a mountain in my office. I could do research onto more and more subjects each month, using what was told to me was Boolean Logic. Now, there was a George Boole in the 1800's who developed this logical system, really quite simple—to other people—with which, of you want to be one of those people, you can understand the operation of computers.

I sound literate, but don't be fooled, I am not. A couple of good friends, my age, just won't buy computers, fearing they would be found out not to be literate. Don't they know they could be just like me, just E-mail, write stuff (as you are seeing), and Google. Boolean Schmoolean!

I am so irritated that they won't join up so we could keep in closer touch. E-mail is wonderful for that. All my children discuss with each other—books, gossip, jobs, activities, what's happened with Mom and each other, plans to meet. One of the joys of motherhood is the keeping of relationships among the children, and, of course, with me. I am in the loop!

Not everything technical pleases me, though, nor do I understand much of it. Take the DVD, the TI-VO, especially the rotten cell phone. Here I am out of the loop, as I can't make mine work, and I resent them all.

People all over the world are giving up all community except virtual, going about in city streets immune from other people next to them, their neighbors even. How do we expect to create the global community if we are giving up the local? How do we expect to understand people next to us if we are always away, knitted into other venues and only loosely hooked to our own environment?

It is weird, surreal, even, to be among people who have to have these things clutched to their ears, and are essentially absent.

Manners toward other people are destroyed by cell phones and by the ubiquitous Blackberry. I have gotten into cars with women, who immediately call on the phone to someone else, as if I were not there. I have spent whole evenings with couples who each have a Blackberry, and they are both bent over them and never see my face.

The medium is the message, indeed.

10 | Old Fogydom

I have always thought that I have avoided being an old fogy. I listen to jazz music with pleasure, not quite as much as with classical music, to be sure. I listen to rock when I am in the mood. I loved *Walk the Line.* I wear skirts just below the knee. I would wear shorter skirts, which I did the last time they came around, but I am not as proud of my knees as I used to be. I read all the well-reviewed up-to-date novelists, and, when I can understand them, I like them. Jennifer Egan, Jonathan Foer, Sadie Smith.

I am not stuffy, in matters of when to serve meals, what to eat, and what to wear. I do prefer non-vegetarian meals, but experiment with everything. I don't like the uniform nature of jeans, and hate jeans at the opera or in restaurants. I love family meals at the dining table, but don't deplore junk food eaten on the run. I think of myself as a perfect combination of ancient and modern. Ha.

Last summer I wrote a perfect *New Yorker* Story. I have sent the *New Yorker* a few non-perfect ones, but have always gotten them back. The closest I have ever come to acceptance was a note, saying "This is good; try *Harpers*." I still have that note, and used to carry it around like baby pictures (or tales of the Displaywriter). In my ancient wisdom I have analyzed the Perfect *NY*-er story down to its last irony, and I have written it! Alas, the *New Yorker* no longer publishes *New Yorker* Stories. Goodbye Thurber, Cheever, Wodehouse, and all that. And again, farewell to me.

I do not understand the ethos of what they publish now. I have tried to define it. Believe me I would copy their ethos if I could. So, I have finally realized that I am, indeed an old fogy. Music and skirts are shallow indicators, *The New Yorker* knows an O.F. when it sees one. Joseph Epstein who is my expert on Seventy, having written an article called "*The Kid is Seventy*" seems not to mind being "out of it," which I guess means old fogydom. Watching from the sidelines, letting younger people go on being "up" on the present and the future. At 91 I feel Joseph Epstein is very much "in"; I am beyond the pale. Die Zeitgeist n'est pas moi.

I don't feel comfortable there, but it does make me cautious and careful what I say. Even what I feel. Remember, "They" live in a different world. The New World.

I remember when I was a 'they' and I have indeed changed since then. The only trouble is that I have a sneaking suspicion that I was correct about some things back then. It reminds me of an often-quoted canard that says it is natural for a youth to be liberal, a protester against the status quo, but if he doesn't become a conservative when he grows up, he is stupid.

It's a canard.

Stupidity can't be said of all youthful attitudes and behavior, but surely it can be said of those that mark a person with little responsibility or obligation. I hate to think of some of my friends shooting out streetlights with a BB gun, but were friends wrong to refuse crossing a picket line? Each case has to be looked at on its own.

Take that famous non-conformist, Albert Einstein, who persisted in his non-conformity into old age. Who would wish he had turned conservative?

Does this mean I forgive the *New Yorker*? You...you *New Yorker*, you watch out. You don't want us old fogies? I might just give up and leave you to your inness. Probably not.

Be tough. Keep trying.

11 | The Neck

Tennessee Williams' *Cat on a Hot Tin Roof* would call me a "little no-neck monster." I used to measure five feet six, and be one of the tallest girls in my class. I always had to play the boy when we paired up to dance. My neck has gotten shorter with all of me; gravity has won. I was gratified to read that four inches off is true of the winner of the Nobel Prize in literature at about my age (Doris Lessing).

Face it, all the skin at 91 is questionable as skin. It looks like parchment. Worse, legs, which are supposed to be the last things to go, well, they went. Dry skin, crackly skin, spots. When I read Nora Ephron's book, *I Feel Bad About My Neck,* it occurred to me that the Nora Neck hasn't lived compared to mine. All she says about chicken necks, elephant necks, wattles, wrinkle. Creepy, loose, scrawny, stringy necks, 91 has, writ large.

She doesn't mention my bete noir, cords. Skin-covered cords running from about two inches under the chin on each side, down to two small projections of the collarbone. Cords that are like bones, growing to restrict movement of the head, though they don't, really.

"Product" can help the facial skin. A large proportion of our national production is skin products, and they can conceal wrinkles and spots pretty well, if you only go out at night. Cords are unconcealable.

You might disagree, thinking of Nora Ephron's suggestions--turtleneck sweaters, Mandarin collars. Unless these things are high enough to choke you, the tops of the cords are going to peak out.

I want to suggest that we eschew turtlenecks, here at 91, in favor of an even immodest cleavage. Now, cleavage is skin, and shares the occasional parchmental everywhere else, but nature's way to protect us is to make men as blind as we are. They will never notice it, so grateful are they for the cleavage. And, cleavage draws attention from cords.

Remember that funny movie in which Diane Keaton falls for Jack Nicholson, *Something's Gotta Give*? When they are about to make love, he protests her turtleneck sweater. In fact, she wears a lot of them, and he protests them all. They scissor it. Good idea. Besides, turtlenecks wreck your hair.

It may be different, way back at Sixty-five, of course.

12 | My Life in Hair

It is odd that I don't feel sorry for bald men; hair is so important to me. I have been in love with two, or perhaps three, bald men, and only in love with one who then had a full head of hair. My love has been pure for all of them. Two of the bald ones didn't even realize that they were bald. I am, of course, speaking of those with a token patch in front, but clearly it was a question of wishful thinking. Or simply semantics? Both have said to me, after some indiscretion of mine, "But do you really think of me as bald?" Of course not.

When women are bald or balding, where the scalp shows through the hair, it is a different matter. They know. To me it is infra dig for a woman to wear a wig unless she has cancer. Men are usually ashamed to, on the theory that "real men" don't think about their appearances. It would be "girly", according to one of the handsomest fully-haired men in Hollywood.

Women know how many hairs are on their heads, and miss each one that gets away. Each one is a divine gift. I am not bald, but deeply fear baldness, from my threatened haired perch.

I have always hated my hair. Now I see this as punishable hubris, but it must be said that my hair was my enemy from the time I was aware of it. "What happened to your pretty curly hair, Dear?" Well, it straightened and it was fine. Fine. Salon-keepers hated it as much as I did. The climax came in Spain, at a salon reputed to be frequented by the wife of Franco. The first operator stayed just five minutes, and fled from the room. A second operator came, spoke rapid Spanish, and said she would call the manager. The manager came, saw the problem, and said to a listening salon, "Muy fino, muy fino." They washed, but refused to set.

The width of an average human hair is approximately 80,000 nanometers. A nanometer is smaller than a living cell and can only be seen with the most powerful microscope. My hairs are smaller than the average hair, by nanometers. You do see the problem, I know, without the help of my data?

In the teen years I tried to curl my hair by sleeping on bobby pins, the pins holding down little swirls of hair. This was uncomfortable and God forbid there was a fire alarm so people could see the plucked chicken, which was my head.

The hair curled. On a dry, cool day the curls lasted until almost lunchtime. In summer it didn't work; they opened like little fists unclenching, right after breakfast.

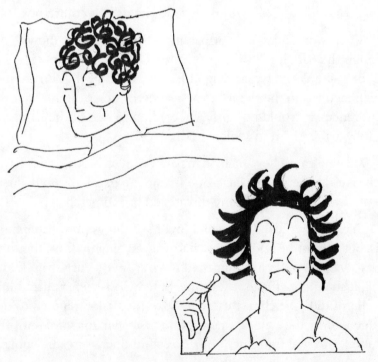

When I got married, I didn't bobby pin. Shortly thereafter, in the suburbs, I began a regimen of hair-house appointments. (This is what a beloved friend, Betsy Cronkite, called them. To preserve her memory I never say "salon" anymore.)

I began to have permanents, which curled the hair chemically.

All this took an inordinate amount of time, but I became fixated on my hair. I saw a chance to retrieve my lovely curly hair. It sort of worked, because of "product": mousse, crèmes, sprays, conditioners, and so on.

The fixation got away from me, and it ended up badly. One day, sailing off Cape Cod with my first husband and a young woman guest, the guest dove overboard, for fun. I thought my husband would be angry, what with all that coming about and jibing over and pulling up right next to her. But he just said, "There's somebody who doesn't worry about her hair." He said it admiringly, and picked her up soaking wet. The vixen!

The next day I cut my hair, so much as to look like Marie Antoinette on the tumbrel going to the gallows. That was a mistake, too. My fine hair couldn't take it. I cut off more, and made bangs, which were too uncomfortable. Straight, straight and ear-showing was that hair, not showing the casual insouciance of that vixen at all.

I grew my hair long again, and tied it back into a ponytail, as most young girls I see doing today. We sailed a lot, jumped overboard for fun a lot, and could go right out to dinner upon coming in from racing. No more problems, with hair.

There were other problems. I married a new husband and became a corporate wife in my fifties. I returned to the hair-house, this time in New York, at Kenneth. There was Mary Farr. Mary Farr "did" some Kennedys, some movie stars, a famous newspaper editor, and me. I had written a letter of application, supplying names for recommendation, explaining "muy fino". I felt lucky. Mary knew how to deal with it, with the help of product. It was an improvement over the suburbs' hair-dos, but putting your hand on it all fixed, it felt like the under side of an oval plastic bowl.

A few years in, my husband gave a dinner for the Museum of Television and Radio, of which he was a board member. Because he was, we were both given movie stars as dinner partners. My dinner partner was Dustin Hoffman. Now, Dustin Hoffman is famous for being nice. I later read a novel by Herman Wouk, called "*A Hole in Texas,*" in which Dustin Hoffman appeared as a very nice character, as he does in my book. His presence was princely. His character served as a party companion to the heroine. He said, among other things, "Your wife is a real savant…" Herman Wouk must have known him.

My experience was different. He interviewed me. Now, I had a long career of interviewing jobs. I was in advertising a couple of times. I was a sociologist of the interviewing and statistical kind. My first interview was with homecoming soldiers of the Second World War, at their homecoming ship, just as they arrived home, hoping to see me, of course, with my clipboard and questionnaire at the ready. I have interviewed hundreds of people. No one has ever before interviewed me.

Dustin Hoffman seemed interested in my family background, my jobs, my friends, and my romance with my second husband. Oh, come on, he was interested. He is a fine actor, but (maybe because of that) I felt his interest. The dinner sped by, he had to leave quickly. He stood. He smiled gloriously. He had enjoyed the evening. I looked adoringly up at him, and he laid his hand on top of my head. To tousle? To pat? He was feeling the plastic bowl.

He didn't pat; he didn't tousle. He looked surprised. It had looked like hair.

Shortly after, I grew my hair long again, eschewed the perm, and wore a pony-tail, with some lavish scrunchies and clips and bows. It wasn't the same, though. I did not have the old young face I had had when I reveled in the severity of long, straight, pulled-back hair.

I go to the hair-house when I am in need of glamour, if you can call it that. I have a short bob, pulled back over my ears, and I submit to my every-six-week brown rinse.

The Truth

I have to tell the dreadful secret. I "comb over". Not like Donald Trump does, or like those men who have only two or three hairs left to comb over a bald pate. I hate what happens when I sleep on my back, which is much of every day, "twenty-four-seven." I forget to look in a rear-view mirror. This last is, by the way, one of the biggest mistakes old women make, that is not knowing what the rear view is like.

The hair cutter always laughs when I mention my fear of baldness, and says it is only a cowlick. The hair parts in the middle of the back of my head, and makes me look as if I have alopecia. What's more, a couple of weeks after my rinse, the part is whitening!

So I am forced to comb over. It is hard to describe, which Trump never has, and won't, but basically I take the comb to the right-rear of the head, and comb that hair to the left. A clip holds it there.

The Saving Grace

Hats. They obviate constant hair-house visits, hide a too-flat top, and keep the hair from blowing and sticking to the face, or creeping into the eyes. Plus, a handsome hat will jazz you up.

I wear a hat almost every day and some evenings if the hair situation is bleak. In some venues I am known as "the hat lady"; there are people who say they don't recognize me hatless.

Hardly anyone knows that, at night or at naps, I wear a hat in bed.

Even during radiation

I always read before sleeping and after some ninety years, I haven't managed to light my page without putting a peripheral glare in my eyes. How does one do this without wearing a hat? People get a rude shock when they enter my bedroom. Most of them gasp.

I watched President Ford's death ceremonies, including the family-and-friends reception. It was a windy day in Grand Rapids. Standing and waiting, women were blown. Their hair, which had been achieved at hair-houses that morning, with their mousses and sprays, blew like sheets drying on the line, straight out, wasting all their pain, money, and time which a hair-do involves.

This didn't need to happen. They could have worn hats, which admittedly destroy hair-dos. We used to wear hats at all events like this, and in church, to honor God. This was the President, after all.

Some Basic Wisdom

You deserve some of the basic wisdom elders are supposed to have, after putting up with all the hair lore. When you begin to wonder whether or not you should wash your hair, you should. Immediately. Otherwise the indecision will never leave you, and will drive you mad.

Try to stay out of hair-houses. They are not ego-building.

13 | Unfirmities

It is lucky that wearing clothing is our cultural default, because the body, at 91, is unfirm. Not roundly, cozily, appropriately firm, over the bones. It is not just those universal flags flopping under the upper arms; every bone has its flags. Hold any bone up in the air to inspect it, and skin falls down from it, not as much as it does under the arms but noticeably.

Bones used to be covered neatly and firmly with …meat. This interior meat has shrunk, now, viv a vis the epidermis, so that the body seems to be covered not in flesh but in an old skin bag. This just happens. There is no choice, I believe. Maybe if I had started earlier to exercise?

One remembers how in childbirth the epidermis used to shrink around what existed inside. When pregnancy occurred, skin expanded, elastically, to cover the stomach. When pregnancy was over, the skin gradually accommodated itself to the lack of bulge; slowly but inevitably it shrank. At 91, well post-pregnancy, it does not shrink around the stomach, or the backside, or the hips, or the arms and legs. Ours is the old skin bag.

Now, one has to wonder what would happen to older woman if we should extend childbirth into the seventies and beyond, as we have extended it currently into the fifties and sixties, adapting technologically to make old age more and more capable. Would we cease to shrink, as we have now, and in the case of childbirth carry around with us that even bigger old skin bag for the rest of our lives?

The Special Case

The buttocks are a special case. It has always been hard for me to use the word, I suppose because of the insistent pairing of the buttocks with the genital organs. I never use the short form, either. Oddly enough, my dictionary seems to have a problem with buttocks as well; the word doesn't appear in my dictionary in between "button" and "buttress." "Buttocks" does appear in the second meaning of "rump" having to do with only animals: "the upper rounded part of the hindquarters of a quadruped animal." It is understandable that I and my dictionary don't use the word much: it is not even human.

I am getting better, or worse, at speaking unspeakables, as current young people have become unburdened with them. But, they still, in my mind, represent the things they technically stand for. One has to detach such words from the things represented and convert them into imprecations, as the youth does, in order to use them comfortably.

My long-deceased, wife-celebrated father was a doctor, and he affected technical or scientific terms for unspeakables, on the theory that this removes their stigma. I was taught technical terms, but in those days I was encouraged never to use them in public. When my first child came along, he was taught to say, "I have to urinate," and others, but he wasn't forbidden to use them. It caused a spate of embarrassed laughter every time he said such things, hilarity which would not have been brought about by "I have to pee", so, together with its cousin words, "urinate" lapsed.

Back to the buttocks, so to speak. Some years ago I read all of Simone de Beauvoir's books, starting with *The Second Sex*, because I thought she was so intelligent on a range of subjects. In one of her books, or in an article, there was a veritable dissertation on the buttocks, in which, to my surprise, she expressed an extreme dislike of the thing, not, I think, of hers specifically, but in general. Female buttocks. She felt this body part hugely disadvantaged women, being so unfirm, peculiarly and variously shaped, embarrassing, especially compared to men's. Do, indeed, men's buttocks stay firm, in comparison to females? Surely, most men do not have the enviable "bubble-butt" which his colleagues attributed to the dancer Jacques D'Amboise. Are men embarrassed to death by their buttocks, especially but not exclusively in old age, as women reputedly are, according to Beauvoir?

Unfortunately, I have not retrieved the exact mini-dissertation on the female buttocks which I dimly remember reading. I've been through *The Second Sex* again, and I have gone to Google, entering the two parts of my research: "Simone de Beauvoir" and "buttocks", and reading through surprising hundreds upon hundreds of references to the pair.

I have found a few interesting things there, as you would too. She explains why women's buttocks are so sexy for men, namely that "the buttocks are the part of the body with the fewest nerves, where the flesh seems an aimless fact." H'mmm. What she says the buttocks are called in other countries, say in Northern Nigeria, where it is "cuwaiwai". What two references say about de Beauvoir's own figure? One says she has "her rather elegant upper half," and "sturdy buttocks and legs." But another speaks of her "lean shanks tanned a rich brown, bony buttocks encased in scarlet trousers." Also h'mmm.

My feelings about the buttocks are not as strong as I believe hers were, but as mine softened towards 91, (my feelings, not the buttocks,) I became more sympathetic. I feel that we don't use our control of clothing as we could. Obviously we have to wear pants in order to do the jobs or play the games we can at 91, and we don't even have to wear those floppy trousers Kate Hepburn wore. We just have to wear blouses or sweaters which fall beneath the hips, so the…well, the derriere, the backside, the fanny, the tush, the heinie--- I can't say b------ one more time. So that body part is concealed, in all its unfirmity.

It occurs to me that I am becoming an unbecoming "just

below" person. Skirts just below the knee, haircuts just below my unfirm Confucian ear lobes, which I forgot to mention, and now blouses just below the b------.

There are a few, very few, women, ---I would like to have told de Beauvior this---who have the female version of the Jacques D'Amboise figure. Those few "bubble-butted" women can compete for beautiful men, or any men, with this body part displayed. Here is a word for you: having well-shaped b------ is called, in some quarters, "callipygian."

The Callipygian Awards

But face it; these callipygian women ought to be ashamed of themselves. They ought to "just below" it like the rest of us. Callipygian' advantage over all the rest of us women is too unfair. They should nobly refuse to use it, like ones turning down their grandfather's trust fund in order to rise in the world just on character and hard work. I am sure there are examples of this for callipygians to emulate.

Finishing off "Unfirmities," with no little relief, let me inject a positive note, which comes from a period even older than 91, the First World War. Remember:

"Pack up your troubles in your old skin bag;

And smile, smile, smile.

What's the use of worrying,

It never was worth while, so

Pack up your troubles in your old skin bag,

And smile, smile, smile!"

Here's good advice: that's all you can do, alas.

14 | Sex, Old

Love goes where it will, Woody Allen said, in explaining his marriage to a near-child. And sex includes love, and vice versa, to most members of my generation.

I want to tell you about my love/sex life in all of its glorious and punishing detail. Would you like to hear about a magic carpet ride of a second marriage, an unbelievable but interesting, hideously painful ending of a first marriage and a helpless fall into love at an advanced age, indeed?

Second Marriage

Well you won't, because I can't tell. There are two kinds of memoir readers; the ones who leap over all the chapters to land on Sex, and those who tastefully skip it. These latter are younger people---well at least younger than the old sex-committers. The latter include all my children and grandchildren, who seem to find Old Sex disgusting, to say the least, destructive of role models, and producing of horrible mental photographs.

Well, sex is quirky, frankly all sex which is not purposefully leading to reproduction. (Let's face it, even that is quirky.) If not quirky, then certainly worthy of "more study". This makes it fascinating, of course. But I don't want to lose my 20-50 year-olds, nor my first writing coach's first rule, which was to banish everything in your work, which embarrasses you, no matter how delicious, brilliant, or educative.

That's it. Believe me, I'm sorry.

15 | Reading

I am happiest when reading. All day on holidays, every evening into night, parts of mornings. But reading has changed. For me there has been a sea change and a see change. And again, these happen.

The big sea change is that now I don't remember what I have read. Oh, I read on, not discouraged by that, but it is different. I used to read mainly to learn, acquire knowledge, and seek stories for conversational gambits. Now I read for the sheer pleasure of the moment. I am tempted to call reading a "thing in itself"; like Emanuel Kant's "*Ding an Sich.*" In the facts that my senses don't add to it, and that I don't really understand it.

The experience of reading itself is just as good as it always was; maybe better, since one doesn't feel obliged to use it. Occasionally some specific thing stays with me. For example, in reading *Mayflower*, by Nathaniel Philbrick, I will probably long remember that there were at least two female sachems, a great revelation to me. I thought Indians were hopelessly male chauvinistic. For another example, reading Walter Isaacon's *Einstein*, I was impressed enough to e-mail my youngest son in Alaska to tell him that Einstein's Ph.D. thesis involved viscosity. My son's job is to find and extract viscous oil, which in nature lies somewhat above petroleum in the ground.

An advantage of the new experience is that now I own at least twice as many books as I can read. I'll never run out, because, of course I don't remember that I've read them. I reread an entire Martha Grimes before I came to the part about a big dog that liked to tease a mother cat by gently moving one of her kittens from the dresser drawer where she had laid them to a different place in the room, for example, the log carrier by the fireplace. Who could forget the panic of that mother, the satisfaction of that dog?

One day I saw in the newspaper a review of a new Michael Connelly. I was amazed that he could have another book out so soon after I had just read a new one, so I walked, on my cane, into town to buy it. The new book was a paperback, whose title I hadn't remembered, but which I had read, *Echo Park*.

At the risk of sounding like a Pollyanna one still learns something almost every day. Now they publish new reviews of a book when it comes out in paperback.

One other difference in my reading is the see change. Spectacles or none, there is blurring, as if someone had smeared oil on my lenses. There is also some skipping. I find myself on a line below where I am supposed to be, or repeating the line above. I just soldier on, but I do make some contributions to texts, after all...For example, I often find a character who has bought a new cat. That's right down my alley, if you'll pardon the expression. But to find that he drives the cat? One thinks of driving in the sense of herding, but... it is a tip-off.

Or, your hero is just risible behind the garage. He's funny? No he's not. Sometimes it takes two or three sentences to sort that out.

One big advantage of the New Reading is that I can read science books now, without guilt. Of course, I don't remember, but I couldn't really learn anyway, so before 80 or 90 or about then, I pretty much had to leave science alone. Now I have "read" Damasio's *Descartes' Error*, about consciousness, but not his following book. I have "read" Dr. Greene from Columbia University on *The Elegant Universe*, but not his following book. I have "read" Dawkins on *the selfish gene*, but not his no-God book.

You already know how much I enjoyed *The Hole in Texas*, which had Dustin Hoffman in it. Well, it was totally about science, a novel about science, specifically the Higgs boson, which the *New York Times* called *The God Particle*. I was in heaven; science plus fiction but not science fiction. Mr. Wouk has a brother who works as a scientist, who must have coached him well; for I thought his description of the Higgs Boson was as good as the *Times'*. It made me feel like a "member of the wedding" (science), or at the very least, "at play in the fields of the Lord."

In case you think I am a closet nerd---oh, how I wish I had been one! Nerds must be so happy, so many unnecessary things are unnecessary to them. Well, I know nerds, and I am no nerd. I started on Nancy Drew and ended up on Philip Craig, the Martha's Vineyard mystery writer. I own two or three times as many Phillip Craig's now, which I read with joy. What a clever man; what a happy life. I grieve that it is over. I just bought his cookbook, Delish!

I like science fiction, too. Looking way, way back, my first husband was a S.F. lover and one day early in the marriage he received his copy of *Astounding SF.* It was devoted to Scientology. L. Ron Hubbard, the magazine editor wrote it. He was an adept. We read it aloud to each other, first one, and then the other. I have to admit that we "bought" it, for the moment.

In between science and mystery, I have new favorite books. They change often. They are legion. It would be like describing all my cats. I'll mention a book that lasted three seasons of being the favorite: Vikram Seth, *An Equal Music.* I am in the middle of Colleen McCullough's five-book series on ancient Rome. I think with pleasure of all the hilarious works of Peter DeVries. I would love to give you a taste of him. When the U.S. astronauts first went aboard the moon, the *New York Times* invited a few New Yorkers to comment on the event. Peter DeVries said, on the first page of the *Times,* "I always knew we were put here on earth for a reason."

Verlyn Klinkenborg. The *Times,* said he re-reads as much, I believe, as I do, for different reasons. One, because he is in love with the books and two, since it becomes a different book because he becomes a different person. This may apply to me too, though my main reason for re-reading is forgetting.

I could go on. I started reading at five or six years old, so I have been reading assiduously for 85 years. Flatly contradicting my statement of pleasure in reading without remembering is that my only serious wish is that at the end of my life I could remember everything I have ever known in the 91 years. (Of course, not just in books.)

I don't have to tell you to read. It happens, too.

16 | Life-Long Anathemae

Anathema I: Other people

Hell, according to John Paul Sartre is Other People, and, of course, I am Other to everybody else. I admit to being sometimes Hell, so I cannot complain about Them.

Well, there is just one awful thing I am sure I don't do. Ay, there's the rub. As soon as you are sure you don't do it, be sure that you may do it. But, please, I am no angel; let me speak of just one thing people do that I hate.

They define themselves thus: "You know me; I don't have a jealous bone in my body." Or a competitive bone, even a mean bone. This is the bone that sticks in my craw, because it is usually the bone that they consistently trip over, right? You can be almost sure that jealousy, or competitiveness, or meanness are traits that people fear they have in spades.

I would so like to attack at this point, but wait. Maybe it is just an indication that they particularly loathe jealousy, meanness, competitiveness. Does his statement mean that this person is actually afraid that this miserable trait (maybe not competitiveness) is attacking him, and his statement means that this person is fighting it?

You can't win, by losing your temper, deploring Other People's faults-which-may-not-be-faults-at-all. But, you know me; I am afraid that I don't have an angel bone in my body!

Anathema II: The Eyes have Had it

Bones are too dangerous. I have other anathemae. Anathemeyes, actually. The almost universal misuse of the eye in literature. The eye has assumed a role in descriptions of people which it is unfit to assume. Show me a novelist who doesn't make people whom he likes' eyes twinkle, and I will show you a very careful user of the English language. Do French, Italian, Dutch eyes twinkle?

Well, American eyes do not. It is true that eyes can be more or less wet, or dry, and if light shines on watery eyes-well, water reflects light, and with a huge leap of wishful thinking, one can see the eyes twinkling. Or shining, or glistening. Very dry eyes won't twinkle. Get 'Tears' before you go out on a date if you want to twinkle.

Even my favorite authors take this shortcut; they do not consider that if a person's eyes give off sparkles, there is something wrong with them. You could be burned.

One of my favorites saw "her granddaughter's eyes shine in the dusk." I don't think so.

Consider diamonds, which are also said to sparkle. Even diamonds displayed at Cartier and Tiffany need carefully-placed brightly-shining lights focused directly on them to give the illusion that they shine. I'm sure only movie stars can afford to light their eyes so they seem to shine. It would be cheaper to pour water into them first. Do they?

What writers are doing, actually, is to use the eye as a metonym, like using "wheels" for "a car." In saying eyes shine or twinkle you are implying happiness, gaiety, pleasure, without having to specify which, but an emotion. I suppose this is a small thing and you can forgive it, though I can't. Now, when I come across a twinkling eye-which I do many times per day of reading-I can't help wondering what's wrong with that eye, or how much better an emotion could be expressed.

Do go ahead, forgive "sparkling." But "eyes glittering with intensity"? Do you believe "There's wisdom in this man's eyes"? Or "Thoughtful eyes"? Or "A twinkle just short of a wink"? How about "mischievous glint", or "indifferent eyes"?

There is real drama, even evil, in eyes. Do you believe "Her hard eyes." "The woman's eyes as full of low cunning and evil intentions as the eyes of a gull." That writer is dangerously anti-gull.

Here is one I admired: "arching his eye-brow almost to his hairline, and raising his wrinkled eyelids, he opened his eyes wide." Now that makes sense (only eyes don't open).

I worked up quite a case on eyes, (and a collection of atrocities,) and actually planned writing a small monograph on "the eyes as metonym", really surprised that no one had already done it. But one day in a house full of books which someone else had collected, I came across an old Ruth Rendel, 1998, and I opened it as excited as I always am to get at a new Rendel.

This was Barbara Vine, actually, her alternate name. Called "*The Chimney Sweeper's Boy.*" The very first words in Chapter One were these: "*It is an error to say the eyes have expression. Eyebrows and eyelids, lips, the planes of the face, all these are indicators of emotion. The eyes are merely colored liquid in a glass.*"

Well said. The first chapter, in fact the entire book, never again mentions this issue, never explains why she brought this up. No shots were heard, no flags went up, not my kind of fuss was made about it.

Well, she did say that her statement about eyes was written by "A Messenger of the Gods."

(Check Chapter I, page 2, et.al.)

Anathema III: Cars

Human beings, or other beings, are not sufficiently evolved to handle automobiles. They are not intelligent enough, nor are they emotionally controllable enough to make possible the use of automobiles on public roads. Something safer must be invented. Cars must go.

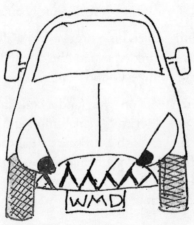

Anathema IV: The Natural

I have been suspicious of The Natural since I was a young mother. I was caught red-handed and vilified twice in one week, for playing on the floor with my first child and his (now called) play-date. The first time the mother-of-play-date came early to pick her son up, and there we were, me proudly showing the two little boys my cherished antique toy, my 30-year-old Lincoln Logs (invented in 1916). With which you could build a small house, very plain, like Lincoln lived in.

"What are you doing," she said. "Playing with them? You had my kid over so he could play with your kid, so they could play with each other. Kids play with kids; adults have time to do adult things. What you're doing is not Natural!"

I think, in fact I know I apologized, using the Lincoln Logs as
my excuse, but I was hot under the collar, as we said then at least in
the Mid-West. They were interested, we were having fun. It wasn't
Natural?

The second mother lived next door, so I had plenty of time
to get up off the floor, but there was evidence. We had been playing, well, wasn't I just showing them how to play? —with those
wonderful wooden train tracks and trains. You can hook together as
many pieces as you can buy, and if you are a would-be engineer you
can make a world of tracks, bridges, back-of-the-yard activities—a
paragon of complexity.

The mother admired our work, and then she sort of gasped.
"You made it! You were playing with them, weren't you? No fair.
They are supposed to learn by doing, not shown by example, and
I'm supposed to be home working or—taking a little time off, for
Heaven's sake. It's just not—and we chorused—Natural"!

I had no excuse this time, but I never forgot my introduction to
The Natural, and my feeling of chagrin.

That was some fifty years ago, and, looking back on it, I am for-
tified by pictures of adults preparing their children for scarce places
in "the best pre-schools." Which will of course get them into the
best kindergartens, which will lead them to the best everything else
in life, which will make them—what? —"successful?" All those men
and women, passing cards in front of their miniature learners so that
they can learn to identify something they might be tested on to put
them ahead of the next child put before the examiner.

This picture doesn't look Natural? Well, I am afraid I would be
doing the same thing if my children had stood a chance of "getting
ahead." I am not proud of this, but it is Natural for our time and
place, read "eras" and "social place" as well as physical, isn't it?

The Natural is not an absolute; it is all relative to these things,
time and places. Can I stop feeling guilty about playing with my

children? Now, you can expect me to go on justifying, giving tren-
chant examples, but it will be more difficult than it was for eyes.

As humans we have spent untold time and money trying to find
out what it is, The Natural, to our Human Condition, which we
have come to call our lives. Looking over my shelf of books, I see
Human Nature writ large. A six hundred plus page book called *H.N.*
by The President's Council on Bioethics, dealing with writings from
"Natural Imperfection and Human Longing" to "Human Dignity".
Send for this; it's free.

Next to it is "*The Human Touch*" (not yet read), by the funniest
playwright ever to emerge. One thing we know for sure about the
Touch is that you better laugh at it, because you are in it for good
or evil. Michael Frayn.

Right next to that is "*The Denial of Death*", which I have read
avidly. Becker has spotted narcissism and a deep need for self esteem
as natural to just-borns and basic to human life. Then comes "*Forbidden Knowledge*", which I am just finishing.

This book, while correctly named, makes me think of man as
computer. It sounds like there are defaults of human behavior which
there are reasons not to pass. Think of Adam and Eve. Roger Shat-
tuck, the author has done, revealingly. But this book has led me
into many "what ifs", which I believe are typical of old people, if
they are lucky and free of daily concerns, and free to think. I was
encouraged in this by the (perhaps temporary) failure of the Cern
superconductor. What if all those brilliant scientists scurrying around
in galactic experiments and mind experiments, like ants building
a factory, well, what if they just aren't supposed to know this stuff?
Forgive me Galileo, F. Bacon, J. Huxley, P. Bradshaw, all you sciento-
philes.

Reading the paper (it happens, today) I see the opening of *The
Bacchae*, based on a famous play by Euripides, reviewed by the *New
York Times'* major critic, reminding me of those feral leavings of our
Darwinian past. The Human Condition. Reminding me of our at-

tempts to help children avoid these leavings for the sake of their and our communal lives. But are those attempts Natural?

Books and plays go on forever in our apparently vain attempt to know the Human Condition. That attempt appears to be our default, trying, trying forever. I have read a pitifully small stack of material over the years. I remember that about twenty years ago there was a spate of books pretending, not proving, to have discovered amazing things in physical anthropology. Ardrey, Tiger, etc. What remains of them for me (see Reading, above) is that a baby's first smile appears because his mother doesn't have chest hair. I will make an effort to find the book. In Google. Under "chest hair" or "baby's smile."

You can see that I cannot banish The Natural. I do feel as if the unknowing love for this thing—these people don't even know that Nature doesn't love us back—is abating. The neighborhood mothers of today would be slower to castigate me. I will let them say "She's a lovely girl, so Natural." It just means "without artifice." It means that in general usage, perhaps.

Still, Oscar Wilde did say *"to be natural is such a difficult pose to keep."*

It would have been best not to apologize. Don't.

17 | The Distinguished Thing

Death. Henry James, delirious on his deathbed, named it thus:
"So here it is at last, the distinguished thing." I hope I remember to
say that, and to feel that way.

You can't help thinking about it, here at 91, as all of your friends
and family disappear. Have you ever heard of Seymour Martin
Lipset, a favorite classmate of mine? To his credit, there were death
notices in several publications and a notable article in *The Econo-
mist* after he died. Oh dear, I thought, I must call our classmates and
reminisce about Marty. I paged through the list in my mind. All of
whom I knew are gone. Boys and girls as they were, as I see them. I
no longer have cohorts.

I check the obituaries often, being selfishly glad when strangers
have died in their nineties or upper eighties. I shiver when they die
under or on my age. I read in detail of the Nobel Prize for literature received by a favorite author, Doris Lessing, who has written
a memoir just recently. She is at least 90, still writing, still healthy.
Hooray!

I don't know which of the abominations listed in S. Nuland's
book; *The Way We Die* is going to knock me down. I think not
knowing is a blessing. As for accidents one can only be endlessly
careful and not worry. I own a Life Support system; you remember
"I have fallen down and can't get up". I never remember to wear
the necklace into which I can talk while lying on the floor, to get
help. Do you think I am "asking for it" (trouble)? I don't; it is just
one more thing to forget.

I am not a Deist, so I have been surprised that I fear hubris, or, as we call it in New York chutzpah. Am I congratulating myself for the horrors I have been spared? I certainly won't list them or any more of my "lucky me's". You have spotted some I have not mentioned? That is deliberate; please don't even think about them!

I have looked up death in a book of quotations. Here is one I can subscribe to, by La Rochefoucauld: *"Everything has been written which could persuade us that death is not an evil-----Nevertheless I doubt whether any man of good sense ever believed it."* I agree with him.

Well, it is possible that scientists are trying to eliminate death, or to put it off for years and years. So many have failed, or are failing, that I am relieved of the pain of realizing that I am missing that grand victory by just a year or two. Here is a study by the Harvard Medical School reported in *Newsweek* in December 2006: *"A compound found in red wine may extend the human life span. A report from the front lines."*

Well, yes. The mice in the study did live longer lives since they received resveratrol, a compound found in red wine grapes.

Controlling important variables, such as diet, these mice were protected against aging-related diseases, such as heart disease, cancer, diabetes, and Alzheimer's, which reduce most people's life span.

Because resveratrol is found in red wine, some people have wondered whether they should drink more red wine, or drink red wine to the exclusion of other alcoholic drinks, but there is not enough resveratrol in red wine: it would take 1,000 glasses to equal the daily dose given to the mice in the study, and we do not yet know whether the tablets and capsules containing resveratrol now sold over the counter are proven of values to humans.

Now I've read a *Nature* article about a new possibility, which has proven able to increase the life span of mice. It is a compound called radamycin first found on Easter Island or Rapa Nui, which gave the compound its name. But believe me; I am not going to just miss the elimination of aging!

I do hate to miss things. First, the development of my grandchildren's lives. Who will they be? I hate to miss what is going to happen in science. I am going to miss most of the discoveries of stem cell research, and already scientists are receiving prizes for them. All those mice, all those fruit flies! Blinding them, taking off their heads, no, I do not allow myself to feel sorry for them. I just want to be in on the results.

Shouldn't we have extra-corporeal gestation? Not just involving other people to carry our babies. If women are going to be more in charge, won't they work to kill all that pain? My best friend says birth pain is proof that God is a man.

Will we ever "speak" with animals? We know they are smart enough. If we ever get past making war, we could afford a grand Apollo-type effort to find out what animals are thinking.

Another bulletin. Two articles in the *NY Times*, one on 6/5/09 called "*Gene by Gene*", the other on 6/4/09 called "*Of Mice and Monologues*" by Mark Lehner. Both reported the isolating of gene

FOX12, including the human capacity for language. Both implied that this was a first clue to the faraway ability of animals to speak. Of course, Disney knew about that.

And, will we ever stop our cruelty to animals? I believe so. I would love to live in the world that had no cruelty to animals. But do deliver us from the organization to protect bacteria! After all, they are made by the force which made us.

As the poet asked, "Did he who made the lamb make thee?"

I can't believe it hasn't happened. Yet.

Extra-terrestrials; living on other planets; the Higgs boson, which will finish off the Way Things Are according to modern physics. I want to know about post-modern physics. I want to know for sure whether we are living in someone else's or some force's computer simulation, as the N.Y. Times described it the other day.

If we are not, I want to know just what is consciousness. Will we know this some day? I will miss it.

I hope my resentment about what I will miss doesn't show. Lord, forgive me my disbelief.

| Afterward

What would I have done differently? First: World War II: I would have moved it to someone else's youth, showing unforgivable selfishness, Dr. Becker's narcissism and need for self-esteem. You can imagine the loss of friends. You can see my classes at Columbia (all or predominantly women and girls). My dates: same as above. There were, of course, shortages. I smoked a small pipe. My aunt sent me bacon and butter by mail from her farm in Iowa, which I kept outdoors on the windowsill and guarded ferociously. Poor me.

Yes, I know the world really suffered. I did not. But, at my age, no men? Men came between me and my textbooks. I worried. I missed men: I missed specific men. There was a smart, handsome young married man in my classes, waiting to be called up. All the girls were a little in love with him. After almost the first year of my classes, he was called. And shortly died. Enough said.

I would not have chosen that war on my time. But there was another related thing, which came between me and my books, the ticking away of that famous biological clock. I was "of an age". Yes, to begin a family. Many years later when I got to know one of my daughters-in-law very well, I saw her life as a perfect schedule, and wrote an article called "*A Modest Proposal for Having it all.*" She had her baby at 18; at 24, over and out, she finished her education and became a lawyer. Nothing bothered her reading, or cried, "there are more important things than this!"

I would like to have had my children earlier, at twenty, say, after two years of college, postponing the rest of my career preparation for ten years. (I had four children, my daughter-in-law had one.) If this seems counterintuitive, I have done it the other way and it kept me from studying.

If a girl and her mate marry at 19, when they are physically at peak but almost out of adolescence, a girl can let herself enjoy motherhood to the full. She can enjoy Little League, which I was too old for, though I didn't actually have to play baseball.

The girl who does it this way can have a fine career at 30-ish. (My mother did starting at 35.) She can finish her education and specialize, and read books without anything else nagging at her, and if she is scholarly, she can go on to be a literary or humanistic nerd. My ideal.

So, no war and early marriage is my advice. There are other, preachy, things I wish I had done. Or not done. I wish I had never done to others what they shouldn't have done to me. I wish I had always reached into adversaries to know what they were thinking, better said, walked in others' shoes. I wish I had been tougher, demanding my "rights", and never never had sought to speak to Aristotle, unless I had miraculously learned to speak ancient Greek.

An Epiphany About The Past

My father. War made me think of him; penicillin makes me think of him, my shortcomings and guilt feelings make me think of him. All this is another story, but we did constantly think of him. My perfect father grew old along with me like Browning's poem said, but his best was not to be. The last of life for which the first was made.

He was as my mother told me he was. No, he didn't die in the war, as many people assumed. A car crash started his dying. He was

in World War I, in a medical division. I have a gold caduceus, on a charm bracelet, which
he had given to my mother. He was a professor of medicine at Johns Hopkins and head of a bacteriology lab, some time involved in seeking out Typhoid Mary. As time went on and I aged, in my mind he did too, and he became more highly regarded and made contributions to his field.

I was happy to meet a current professor of medicine at Hopkins just a few years ago, and I told him, proudly, of my father. He didn't know my father, but he did look him up in the hospital records. There he was, as my mother had described him, with records of his trips, with expense accounts (breakfast, 10 cents, dinner, forty cents.) Best of all, there were copies of letters to my mother and his doctor brother, lavish with praise and missing him.

For the first time, it occurred to me that the éminence grise I had come to "know" had been a boy of thirty-five.

Watch out for the past; it can fool you.

LaVergne, TN USA
24 March 2011
221473LV00001B/1/P